THE WORLD OF MARTIAL ARTS

MARTIAL ARTS AROUND THE GLOBE

BY JIM OLLHOFF

Visit us at
www.abdopublishing.com

Published by ABDO Publishing Company, 8000 West 78th Street, Suite 310, Edina, MN 55439.
Copyright ©2008 by Abdo Consulting Group, Inc. International copyrights reserved in all countries.
No part of this book may be reproduced in any form without written permission from the publisher.
ABDO & Daughters™ is a trademark and logo of ABDO Publishing Company.

Printed in the United States.

Editor: John Hamilton
Graphic Design: Sue Hamilton
Cover Design: Neil Klinepier
Cover Illustration: iStockphoto
Interior Photos and Illustrations: p 1 capoeira artist, iStockphoto; p 5 Buddhist monk, Corbis;
p 6 globe, iStockphoto; p 7 painting of monks practicing kung fu, Corbis; p 8 globe, iStockphoto;
p 9 (top) Greek vase showing pankration, courtesy University of Texas at Austin; (bottom)
Alexander the Great statue, iStockphoto; p 10 globe, iStockphoto; p 11 kalaripayit stylists,
AP Images; p 12 globe, iStockphoto; p 13 Burmese boxers, Corbis; p 14 globe, iStockphoto,
p 15 savate footfighters, Corbis; p 16 map, courtesy Central Intelligence Agency; p 17 police
officers practice silat, Getty Images; p 18 globe, iStockphoto; p 19 Beach/Sombo Wrestling National
Championship, Getty Images; p 20 globe, iStockphoto; p 21 Brian London and Muhammad Ali,
AP Images; p 22 globe, iStockphoto; p 23 (top) Muay Thai boxers, Corbis; (bottom) *Ong Bak: Muay
Thai Warrior* poster, courtesy Golden Network Asia Limited; p 24 map, courtesy Central Intelligence
Agency; p 25 arnis stylist, courtesy Kick Connection, Inc.; p 26 map, courtesy Central Intelligence
Agency; p 27 capoeira performer, iStockphoto; p 28 (top) globe, iStockphoto; (bottom) krav maga teacher
and student, courtesy Krav Maga Worldwide; p 29 martial artist performing a handstand, iStockphoto;
p 31 costumed martial arts masters, Getty Images.

Library of Congress Cataloging-in-Publication Data

Ollhoff, Jim, 1959-
  Martial arts around the globe / Jim Ollhoff.
    p. cm. -- (The world of martial arts)
  Includes index.
  ISBN 978-1-59928-979-3
  1. Martial arts--Juvenile literature. I. Title.

GV1101.35.O55 2008
796.8--dc22
                              2007030549

CONTENTS

武 道

INTRODUCTION

A martial art is any kind of fighting system, usually unarmed. Martial arts can be used primarily for defense, or for attacking, or a mixture of both. Some martial arts began as dances, and grew to become effective tools for fighting. Countries around the world developed many different kinds of martial arts. Each art is unique, and each has an interesting history.

There are many ways to strike an opponent. You can strike with a fist, with an open hand, or with the side of the hand. You can strike with elbows and knees, or you can kick with your feet. You can even strike someone with your forehead. However, this strike, like all strikes in martial arts, is dangerous if you haven't been trained how to do it. Untrained people can easily break their hands, legs, or worse if they do the techniques improperly.

Another way to fight someone is to use leverage to make an opponent lose balance, and then push the opponent to the ground. This is called a "throw," and it is an effective way to control someone. A joint lock is a way to bend a person's joint in a way that causes pain or immobilizes the opponent. Some martial arts teach grappling instead of striking. A grapple is any kind of throw, joint lock, or choke that causes an opponent to submit.

Different martial arts emphasize different strengths. Some emphasize kicking. Others emphasize grappling. In some martial arts, the emphasis is on speed—doing techniques very quickly.

Other martial arts emphasize techniques with a lot of power. Some martial arts favor fighting an opponent very close. Other styles prefer keeping opponents farther away before launching kicks.

Martial arts also have different purposes. Some martial arts were created for use in the military. Some martial arts are performed primarily for sport, while others are taught for street self-defense. Whatever the emphasis or purpose, there is a wondrous variety of martial arts from around the globe.

Above: A Buddhist monk practices martial arts in China.

WHERE DID MARTIAL ARTS COME FROM?

Below: Martial arts may have begun in India and spread north to China, and then moved east to Korea and Japan.

There are many legends about the origin of martial arts. The most popular legends state that India was the birthplace of all martial arts. From there, Buddhist monks took the martial arts to China. In China, the martial arts became well-developed fighting styles. According to the legends, the knowledge of the martial arts then spread to Japan, Korea, Okinawa, and Indonesia.

However, there is little historical evidence to support these stories. It is more likely that martial arts developed at the same time in many places. Tribal warriors and national soldiers probably needed martial arts as they went to war. All over the globe, people had to train to do battle more effectively. Martial arts probably sprang up in many parts of the world independently.

Which country had the first martial art? This is hard to say for sure. In Babylonia (now the country of Iraq), statues of unarmed fighters have been found dating before 2000 B.C. There are pictures from Africa that are even older. They show people who appear to have their arms in a block position, similar to a modern-day karate block. Other figures appear to be wrestling. Do these statues and pictures show martial arts? Or do they show something else? In India, some ancient religious texts use words that seem to mean "fighting." However, other scholars think the words refer to dancing.

It's hard to tell where the first martial art emerged, or how the various martial arts influenced each other. What we do know is that many countries developed unique styles of martial arts. This book looks at a variety of martial arts from around the globe.

Above: A painting of monks practicing kung fu at the Shaolin monastery.

ANCIENT GREECE: PANKRATION

In the 33rd Olympiad, in 648 B.C., athletes competed in a sport called *pankration*. Historians don't know much about this sport. However, we know that it was some kind of wrestling-boxing contest. Contestants wrestled, punched, kicked to the knees, pulled hair, choked, and tried to break each other's fingers. There seemed to be very few rules. A fight could go on for hours unless one of the contestants surrendered or died.

Below: In 648 B.C., athletes competed in the sport of pankration during Greece's Olympiad.

One of the moves used by the contestants was called a stomach throw. A contestant leapt up, grabbing his opponent by the shoulders and placing a foot over his stomach. Then the contestant intentionally fell on his own back while keeping a grip on his opponent. After landing on his back, the contestant flipped his opponent over his head. It could be a brutal throw against an unprepared opponent. Many martial arts still use similar throws today.

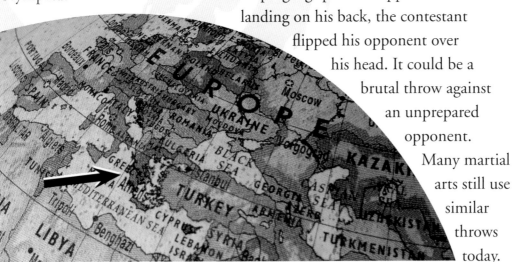

We know little about pankration because there aren't very many written records about the martial art. However, we know that pankration was a martial art that sprang up in one small corner of the world. One legend says that pankration was the first martial art. This legend states that the Greek ruler Alexander the Great (356 B.C. to 323 B.C.) taught pankration to his armies.

After the Greek soldiers invaded India, they taught their martial art to the people of Asia. We know that this legend probably isn't true because historians have records of martial arts in Asian cultures long before pankration was used in Greece.

Above: The sport of pankration came from ancient Greece and was some type of wrestling-boxing contest. Historians are unsure of the exact rules.
Left: A statue of Alexander the Great.

Ancient India: Kalaripayit and Vajramusti

Some people believe that India had martial arts before anyone else. Historians know that ancient Indians did indeed use martial arts. Indian legends even tell of fierce warriors who could defeat elephants or lions. However, this is probably an exaggerated legend, not historical fact.

In southern India, there is a martial art called *kalaripayit,* or *kalarippayattu.* People have practiced this art since 600 A.D., and possibly long before. The word kalaripayit means "battlefield practice." Stylists train for high kicks, low crouches, grappling, and joint locks. They also train heavily with swords, sticks, spears, and knives.

Below: Martial artists learned kalaripayit and vajramusti in India.

By the 1100s, a martial art call *vajramusti* emerged in India. This was a fierce type of striking and wrestling, where contestants often died during fights. The Indian warrior caste, the *Kshatriya* (similar to the Japanese samurai) practiced this art. One of their training techniques was to soak their hands in milk, and then punch a slab of rock (historians aren't sure whether the milk was for religious or medicinal purposes). Vajramusti is no longer practiced today. It may have disappeared when it merged with other martial arts.

Above: Martial artists perform a dagger fight in Mumbai, India. Their ancient style of martial arts is known as kalaripayit, which means "battlefield practice." Stylists train with weapons, as well as learn high kicks, low crouches, grappling, and joint locks.

MYANMAR: THAING

Myanmar has a variety of martial arts that are sometimes grouped under the term *thaing*, which means "self-defense." These martial arts include *bando, banshay, lethwei*, and *naban*. Sometimes these are called *Burmese martial arts*, since Myanmar was once called Burma. Bando refers to an unarmed martial art that emphasizes evasion and quick, up-close techniques. A bando stylist will initially withdraw from an attack, and then execute a devastating counterattack. A banshay stylist practices with weapons, mostly swords. Lethwei emphasizes boxing, and naban emphasizes wrestling.

Below: Thaing developed in Myanmar, a country once known as Burma.

As early as 1000 A.D., martial artists from neighboring India and China were teaching techniques to Burmese monks and royalty. Many historians believe that Chinese martial artists watched animals fight, and then developed fighting styles similar to those animals. The Chinese martial artists came to Burma and brought the animal techniques of the cobra, monkey, tiger, eagle, and others. Burmese martial artists combined the Chinese styles of fighting with their own, and founded thaing.

Thaing became less popular while the British ruled the country from 1888 until World War II, which ended in 1945. The British tried to stamp out the practice of thaing because they were afraid the Burmese people would use it against them.

During the Japanese occupation of Burma during World War II, Burmese martial artists learned many throwing and grappling techniques from Japanese martial artists. This gave thaing a new popularity. Burmese martial artists brought thaing to the United States in the 1960s.

Above: Burmese matches allow the use of hands, legs, knees, feet, elbows, and even the head.

13

FRANCE: SAVATE

In France, there is a martial art called *savate*, also called French footfighting. It is a style that makes frequent use of kicks. In fact, the word *savate* comes from the French word for "old boot."

Historians don't know the exact origin of savate. It appears that sailors practiced savate as early as the 1600s. It may be that sailors learned some kicks as they traveled to Asia. Legend says that the stylists use more footwork because sailors needed to keep their hands on the rails of their ships to keep their balance in heavy waves.

In the early 1800s, there was a movement to make savate a legitimate sport. The savate stylists took many dangerous techniques out of the system, and placed more emphasis on point scoring. They added high kicks and more hand strikes. In 1924, savate was added as a demonstration sport in the Olympic Games in Paris, France.

Today, savate stylists continue to practice it as a sport. Savate is most popular in France. Consistent with their history, savate stylists still wear shoes in tournaments. While most martial arts systems use colored belts to represent the different ranks, savate uses colored gloves.

Below: The European country of France is known for the martial art of savate.

Above: The martial art of savate is also called French footfighting. It became popular in Paris and northern France in the 1800s. This type of street fighting used only kicks. The modern sport of savate was developed further by Michel Casseux and his student Charles Lecour in the mid 1800s. When Lecour was beaten in a friendly match against a boxer, he began training to use punches, as well as kicks. Today, in competitive savate, there are four common types of kicks and punches. The kicks are fouetté ("whip," or roundhouse kick), chassé (side or front piston-action kick), revers ("reverse," or hooking kick), and coup de pied bas ("low kick"). The punches are jab, cross, hook, and uppercut.

INDONESIA: PENTJAK SILAT

The words *pentjak silat* mean "training for combat," but some of the movements are so graceful that they resemble dancing more than martial arts. In fact, pentjak silat stylists sometimes perform dance routines as entertainment at festivals. The dancing, however, conceals techniques that can be very dangerous. Pentjak silat, sometimes shortened to *silat*, is popular in Indonesia and Europe.

Below: The martial art of pentjak silat is popular in Indonesia.

There is an ancient legend about how silat began. According to this legend, a woman went to a stream to fill up her water bucket. While there, she saw a fight between a tiger and a large bird (some legends say the fight was between a snake and a bird that could not fly). Fascinated, she watched the animals battle for hours. Her angry husband, wondering where she was, had been out looking for her. Finally, he found her at the well. Filled with rage and impatience, he tried to strike her.

The woman defended herself with the movements of the animals she had been watching. Both she and her husband were amazed at her new skills, and she began to teach silat.

The emphasis in silat is to strike before an attacker's movement is finished. Because of this, silat stylists need to be very fast. If an attacker starts to punch, the silat stylist will perform a devastating series of strikes and a takedown before the attacker has finished the punch.

Silat teaches a wide variety of defensive and attacking movements, such as throws, kicks, punches, trips, sweeps, joint locks, and chokes. Silat stylists practice their moves until they can respond automatically to possible threats.

Above: Police officers outside their headquarters in Jayapura, Papau New Guinea, practice silat as part of their morning exercise routine. Silat stylists perform super-fast strikes and takedowns.

RUSSIA: SAMBO

Russian martial artists study an art called *sambo*, also called *sombo*. It is an abbreviation for a Russian phrase that means "self-defense without a weapon." Sambo doesn't have a single founder. It began with a number of people in the early 1900s. These founders combined fighting ideas from judo, wrestling, grappling, and joint locks. They weaved in the fighting techniques of neighboring countries, especially Mongolian wrestling. By 1938, Russians recognized sambo as a sport. It became the training style for police, army soldiers, and security guards.

Martial artists often talk about three different kinds of sambo: sport, self-defense, and combat. Sport sambo is for students entering competitions. They fight each other and try to wrestle, grapple, and throw their opponents. Stylists score points when they are able to get their opponents to the ground.

Self-defense sambo is, as the name suggests, for self-defense. Instructors teach people how to defend themselves against attacks. There are no offensive moves in this kind of sambo—it's all about defense.

Finally, combat sambo is the type taught to Russian soldiers and police. It includes throws that are too dangerous for sport sambo, and joint locks that can cause serious injuries. Combat sambo is a dangerous and effective martial art against assailants.

Below: Sambo is a popular martial arts style in Russia.

Above: Two sambo stylists compete in a national championship match.

ENGLAND: BOXING

Boxing can trace its roots to the warriors of ancient Greece, Rome, and North Africa. However, the boxing we know today started in England in the 1700s. Back then, boxers fought with bare knuckles, and there were no weight divisions. There was no ring, no referee, and no time limit. Sometimes people were actually killed in the sport.

In 1743, a fighter named Jack Broughton introduced a set of rules called the London Prize Ring rules. These rules made it illegal to hit a man who was down. The new rules called for padded gloves, referees, and judges. In 1867, those rules were updated and called the Marquess of Queensberry rules. Today, most boxing rules are based on the Marquess of Queensberry rules.

In boxing, contestants fight for several rounds, which last from one to three minutes. Judges award points for solid hits, and the fighter with the most points after all the rounds are finished is declared the winner. Boxers need to duck and weave to avoid getting hit. At the same time, they try to make contact with their opponent. There is a lot of strategy involved in boxing.

In the 1920s and 1930s, Jack Dempsey and Joe Louis were two of the great fighters who dominated boxing. In the 1940s and 1950s, champions included Sugar Ray Robinson and Rocky Marciano. In the 1960s and 1970s, boxers like Muhammad Ali and George Forman thrilled audiences. Boxing continues to be a popular sport today.

Below: The boxing we know today began in England in the 1700s. It was a fierce sport. Boxers fought with bare knuckles and no time limit. Sometimes competitors died during boxing matches.

Above: The popular sport of boxing began in England in the 1700s. In 1966, in London, England, American heavyweight boxing champion Muhammad Ali smashed a right punch into the jaw of his challenger, Brian London of Britain. Ali knocked out his opponent in the third round for his fifth successful defense of the heavyweight championship title.

THAILAND: MUAY THAI

In Thailand and surrounding countries, a martial art called *Muay Thai* emerged. Sometimes called Thai boxing, it has also been called the "Art of Eight Limbs." That's because Muay Thai stylists use not only their hands and feet as weapons, but their elbows and knees as well. In Muay Thai, much of the fighting is in close, so elbows and knees become important weapons.

In the old days, traditional Muay Thai stylists threw hard kicks to the legs, and blocked kicks with their shins. Fighters leapt in with a knee to the head or an elbow to the face. Sometimes, they wrapped rope around their hands and feet. Muay Thai became a sport between two people who fought in front of a crowd. Sometimes they fought to the death. It was a very brutal sport. In modern tournaments, however, Muay Thai stylists wear foam pads and protective gear. They fight with strict rules, time limits, and referees.

Below: The martial art of Muay Thai developed in Thailand.

Legend says that in the 1500s, King Naresuen of Thailand (at that time, Thailand was called Siam) was imprisoned by the army of Burma. The Burmese king told him that he could go free if he could fight 12 of the best Burmese warriors. King Naresuen used his Muay Thai skills to beat all 12 Burmese fighters, and so he was set free.

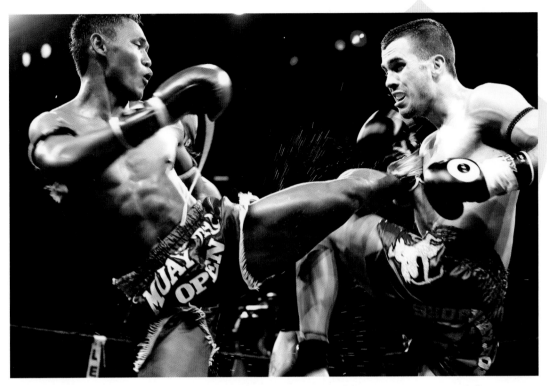

Above: Muay Thai boxers use hands, feet, elbows, and knees as weapons. This sport is sometimes called the "Art of Eight Limbs."

Right: The popular 2005 movie *Ong Bak: Muay Thai Warrior* and the 2006 movie *The Protector* featured Tony Jaa, a Muay Thai stylist. Muay Thai is popular in Southeast Asia, and is a rapidly growing sport in America.

THE PHILIPPINES: ARNIS

The martial artists of the Philippines developed a fighting style that made use of sticks and knives. Different people call this art by different names. Sometimes it is called *arnis de mano*, or the more modern term *arnis*. Sometimes it is called *escrima*, possibly named after the Spanish term for fencing. Outside the Philippines, artists often call the art *kali*. Sometimes, the Philippine martial arts use the acronym *FMA* (Filipino Martial Arts).

In most martial arts around the world, weapons are only used by advanced students. Most martial arts teachers encourage students to master hand and foot techniques before they use weapons. Arnis is unusual because it gives beginning students two sticks, called *escrima sticks*, each about 2.5 feet (76 cm) long. The idea of arnis is to move the sticks quickly, striking or disarming opponents. An arnis stylist can strike multiple times in rapid succession.

Arnis stylists strike opponents with the sticks, using quick flicks of their wrists to add speed to the movements. Typically, one escrima stick strikes high while the other stick strikes low, to the knees or groin. Then, they often switch so that the stick that just struck low moves to strike the head.

Below: The fighting style of arnis developed in the Philippines.

Arnis stylists move their arms up and down as they strike, creating a dizzying flurry of hits. By keeping one stick up and the other stick down, they also protect themselves at the same time.

Arnis stylists learn to use kicks and grappling holds as well. Advanced students practice with a knife and a stick. However, their biggest weapon is the quick use of their two sticks.

Above: Arnis stylists use two escrima sticks, each about 2.5 feet (76 cm) long, to quickly strike or disarm their opponents.

BRAZIL: CAPOEIRA

The martial art of *capoeira* was probably brought to Brazil by African slaves sometime in the early 1600s. Capoeira is a remarkable acrobatic art. Capoeira stylists are in constant motion, performing handstands, headspins, cartwheels, leg sweeps, flips, and head butts. Usually, they kick while doing handstands or other acrobatic movements. Traditionally, stylists practice their art inside a circle of people while music plays. The people clap and sing along with the music as they watch the capoeira stylists. Capoeira, in fact, looks a lot like dancing. If you didn't know better, you might think the stylists were dancing instead of practicing a martial art. Some historians believe that this is how the early slaves practiced. They "hid" their martial art in the form of a dance. When their Brazilian oppressors watched, they thought the slaves were dancing instead of practicing a martial art.

Scholars aren't sure where the word *capoeira* comes from. It might be from the word "rooster," named after the way roosters fight. It might also be from the word "capa," which is a type of hat that African slaves often wore.

Capoeira stylists make more use of their feet than their hands. This may be because the African slaves frequently had bound hands. It may also reflect the need to disguise their art, to make it look like dancing instead of a martial art.

Below: The acrobatic art of capoeira began in the South American country of Brazil.

Africans used capoeira to build community with each other, as well as practice the art. The art grew in popularity until 1890. Then, the government made it illegal to practice because so many criminals were using it. After it became illegal, the artists had to practice in secret. However, in 1928, the government recognized capoeira as a sport, and it began to be practiced openly again. Today it is a growing sport all over the world.

Above: Capoeira stylists use dance-like moves such as handstands, headspins, leg sweeps, cartwheels, and flips.

ISRAELI KRAV MAGA

Above Right: The martial art of krav maga began in Israel.

Below: Krav maga means "close combat." This fighting style is often taught to soldiers and police. It is used in real-life, self-defense situations, not as a sport.

The Israeli martial art of *krav maga* is often taught to soldiers and police. The phrase means "close combat." Krav maga has no competitions, and it is not a sport. All the techniques in krav maga are designed for real-life situations.

Krav maga began in the 1930s. It was developed by a man named Imi Lichtenfeld. He first taught the fighting style to the Jewish community to defend against the Nazis. Krav maga didn't come to the United States until the 1980s.

Krav maga assumes that every fight will be a life-and-death battle. Therefore, instructors teach head butts, groin strikes, and other brutal attacks. Krav maga chooses its techniques based on their effectiveness in real-life combat.

While the combat techniques of krav maga are similar to other martial arts, the training techniques are often unique. Stylists train for worst-case scenarios. They train against multiple attackers. They sometimes train with loud music blasting so they get used to fighting with distractions. They'll also sometimes train with one arm tied behind their back to simulate an injury.

Summary

There are thousands of martial arts, and we've only talked about a few here. We didn't talk about *kurash wrestling* from Uzbekistan, Egyptian stick fencing, Finland's *kas-pin*, Mongolian *boke*, or African *re-efi areh-ehsee*. Most countries and areas of the world have a traditional fighting style.

Many of the martial arts today, especially in the United States, are combination arts. This means that the founder took a little bit from one martial art, a little bit from another, and then mixed it all together and created a new style. In fact, this mingling of the arts is so common that it is often difficult to trace the history of a particular style.

Most countries have a native fighting style. Usually, the fighting style fits with the country's history and culture. Fighting styles are influenced by a country's history and its interactions with people from other countries. In fact, we can often learn something about a country by understanding its fighting style. It's always interesting to seek an answer to the question: "Why did they develop their style *that* way?"

Above: Powerful and flexible, skilled martial artists often use acrobatic moves in their styles.

GLOSSARY

Belt

Most modern martial arts schools use a system of colored belts to rank their students based on their abilities and length of training. Each school decides the exact order of belts, but most are similar in ranking. A typical school might start beginner students at white belt. From there, the students progress to gold belt, then green, purple, blue, red, and brown. The highest belt is black. It usually takes from three to five years of intense training to achieve a black belt.

Joint Lock

A submission technique, often used in jiu-jitsu, judo, and aikido, in which an attacker's arm or leg is twisted and held tight so that a joint, such as an elbow, knee, or ankle, is painfully overextended.

Judo

A martial arts style created by Dr. Jigoro Kano in Japan in the late 1800s. The word *judo* means "the gentle way." Dr. Kano believed his martial art was the gentle way to learn about life. Judo stylists use throws, trips, and falls to overpower their opponents.

Kung Fu

A Chinese martial art that had an early influence on the development of other martial arts worldwide, such as karate. The phrase kung fu means "achievement through great effort."

Monk

A person who lives in a religious community. Monks usually take certain vows, such as nonviolence or poverty, to help them focus less on the distractions of the outside world. Buddhist monks from China's Shaolin Temple were some of the first to use kung fu, both as a method of exercise and self-defense, and as a way to clear the mind.

Okinawa

The birthplace of modern karate. The main island of Okinawa is part of the Ryukyu chain of islands, which are situated in the Pacific Ocean south of Japan. Although it was once an independent nation, Okinawa today is a prefecture, or state, of Japan.

Samurai

The trained warrior class of medieval Japan.

Tournament

A series of contests, usually in a specific sport or game, between a number of competitors. Winners play winners, until only two people are left to compete. The winner of this final competition is the ultimate champion.

World War II

A war that was fought from 1939 to 1945, involving countries around the world. The United States entered the war after Japan's bombing of the American naval base at Pearl Harbor, in Oahu, Hawaii, on December 7, 1941.

Right: South Korean martial arts masters.

INDEX